# The Carver's Daughter

## a memoir

*Kari Jo Spear*

Kari Jo Spear

# Copyright

The Carver's Daughter: A Memoir
Karen Joelle Spear

Copyright ©2020
Karen Joelle Spear

Cover design copyright © 2020 Brooke Albrecht. Used with permission.

Interior design by Dennis Lanpher.

Edited by Katherine M. De Groot.

Print ISBN-13: 978-1-7350799-1-2
Digital ISBN-13: 978-1-7350799-0-5

Front Cover Photos: Hummingbird carving photo © Karen Joelle Spear, 2020. Used by permission. Blackburnian warbler carving © Erin Talmage, 2004. Used by permission.
Back Cover Photo: Photo © Karen Joelle Spear, mid 1970s. Used by permission.
Acknowledgment Section: Photographer unknown, 1981.
Museum History: Photo © Karen Joelle Spear, 2016. Used by permission.
Chapter 1: Photo © Karen Joelle Spear, 2020. Used by permission.
Chapter 2: Photo © Erin Talmage, 2012. Used by permission.
Chapter 3: First Photo © Karen Joelle Spear, late 1970s. Used by permission.
Chapter 3: Second Photo © Karen Joelle Spear, 2020. Used by permission.
Chapter 4: Photo © Karen Joelle Spear, 2020. Used by permission.
Chapter 5: Photo © Karen Joelle Spear, 2020. Used by permission.
Chapter 6: Photo © Karen Joelle Spear, 2020. Used by permission.

*This book is dedicated to my only sibling,*
*the Birds of Vermont Museum.*
*We came of age together, both created and shaped*
*by the force of nature that was our father,*
*Bob Spear*

# Contents

# Acknowledgments

This book, and I, owe so much to the amazing staff of the Birds of Vermont Museum: Erin Talmage, Kirsten Talmage, and Allison Gergely. They helped me pull together the photos, answered my random (and frequent) questions, and most importantly told me that this was worth doing. And they laughed in the right places. Also, a huge thank you to my fellow members of the board of directors, past and present, who give so much to the museum and are always so encouraging.

Thanks to Ingrid Rhind for her constant kindness and patience with my family and me, for all she has done for the museum, and for her continued encouragement of my writing, even though she moved to the other side of the world. And thanks to Deborah Moran and her daughters, Kaitlynn and Hannah, for always holding the museum so closely in their hearts. And, of course, I deeply appreciate my husband, Dennis Lanpher, who always takes time from his drumming to proofread something or accompany me on yet another trip to the museum to double check some detail, and my daughters, Alaria and Crystal, who put up with a birder/writer for a mother and don't complain (too much). They could probably write a book called "The Writer's Daughters."

Thanks to the whole community of birders and museum supporters that I'm so lucky to be a part of.

I deeply appreciate Brooke Albrecht, who created the wonderful cover and was very patient with me.

As always, a huge thank you to my incomparable editor, Katherine M. De Groot, who wields a mighty red pen and always knows what I really mean to say, even when I'm nowhere close.

This book would not have happened without my parents, Bob and Sally Spear. They did so much for me, and still do, even though they have both passed away. Most importantly, they always made me know how much I was loved, despite the fact that we did not live together in the same house for very many years. And I deeply appreciate Gale Lawrence and all the "cultural experiences" she came up with to entertain the teenager (and often the teenager's friends) she was saddled with on weekends, and for putting up with the giggles and tears of a fellow writer as I was hatching.

And thanks to everyone who loves ice cream as much as my father did.

Kari Jo and Bob Spear in Montpelier, Vermont
*Photographer unknown, 1981*

# Introduction

This book would not exist without the Birds of Vermont Museum, which would not exist without my father, Robert N. Spear Jr. Neither would I. I'm an only child, and so I guess that makes the museum my sibling, in an odd way. Certainly we grew up together, the museum and I, through all the throes of childhood and adolescence. I think it's safe to say the museum was more difficult to raise than I was. At least, my father never had to get permits to have me. He just had to buy me a lot of books.

The time I spent with my father was nearly always linked to the museum. Some of my oldest memories are of working beside him to create it. And he, in his quiet way, turned the creation of the museum into life lessons, or life experiences, or whatever it is that fathers share with their daughters.

This book also exists because one summer afternoon, I was volunteering in the museum's gift shop. Erin Talmage, the executive director, walked past the wetland diorama, paused by the loon display, and said, "Kari Jo, we need more material for the next newsletter. Would you write something?"

Normally, I write fantasy novels, not bird things. I must have looked skeptical.

"I don't know. Maybe something about growing up with your father?"

I laughed. "Yeah sure, I could write a book about that."

She just smiled.

So "The Carver's Daughter" ... articles? essays? vignettes? for the museum newsletter, *Chip Notes*, began. I didn't intend to write more than one, but Erin kept politely asking for more, and I kinda fell into a pattern. The museum started getting nice feedback from readers. Then a weird thing happened. When I met fellow birders or was at the museum, people would say, "Oh, you're the Carver's Daughter!" Well, I've always been the carver's daughter, and usually people told me, "We love his carvings so much!" But now they were referring to me with a capital C and a capital D, and adding, "We love your stories so much!" It's a wonderful feeling.

People suggested that I compile the installments into a book. I resisted, thinking how hard it would be to find a publisher for such an odd anthology. But now self-publishing is here, and I figured it wouldn't be hard to create the collection myself. (Ha. Wishful thinking from early in the process!) I didn't realize how much fun it would be to revisit the pieces I'd written over the last eight years.

This book begins with the official Birds of Vermont Museum history, stolen from the museum website (I wrote it, so I'm entitled). It gives background for those of you who don't know about this amazing place tucked away in Huntington, Vermont. Seventeen ... articles? essays?

vignettes? follow, mostly in the order in which they were published in *Chip Notes* from 2011 to 2019.

Were they written to capture the meaning of life, of growing up, of important events? No. They're just memories that popped into my head whenever Erin said she needed another one. There's no great hidden theme. But I think that sometimes chance works to create a whole in a natural, organic way. At the very least, these anecdotes make people smile in this insane world we're living in, and that is a worthwhile thing.

I include a brand-new piece called "My Father and the Camp" that I wrote just for this book. It has never been published anywhere else.

I end the book with a piece that was published in 2015, "Remembrance: Tales of My Father." He passed away on October 19, 2014. A lot of people thought I would stop writing my memories after that. But I was able to carry on—just as the museum is carrying on. He'd planned for it to. I have no intention of stopping, either. In another eight years or so, I'll probably compile another collection. I've got over fifty years of memories, after all.

I consider myself lucky beyond belief to be the Carver's Daughter.

# Museum History

*Taken from www.birdsofvermont.org, with permission.*

Museum entrance
*Photo by Kari Jo Spear, 2016*

The Birds of Vermont Museum exists because of a series of happy accidents. Bob Spear had a dream that was too big to fit anywhere else. He fell in love with Gale Lawrence, who just happened to have a workshop and the foundation of an old barn in her side yard. The land across the road happened to go on sale. Some friends were willing to donate money to the project. People volunteered to help out. And the rest is history.

The museum came together in bits and pieces. It's hard to date when it first started, since the earliest carvings (the parakeets) are from 1938, when Bob was eighteen. At first, all the carvings fit in the workshop, but then Bob didn't have space to carve any longer. Some good friends made a generous donation, and he hired a crew and built a new barn on top of the old foundation in 1981. (Gale called it "the barn" long after he was calling it "the museum.")

By 1987, Bob had carved 321 birds. That's when the official opening was celebrated with champagne, though the place had been sort of open to visitors before then. Bob set up the museum as a nonprofit, asked some good folks he knew to become board members in 1988, and hit the ground running.

Within a few years, he filled up the main floor of the new barn with carvings. So he finished off the downstairs. By 1992, the museum had acquired a viewing window, a real gift shop, a conference room, offices, central heating, and most importantly, bathrooms. (This was so people didn't have to keep running up to Gale's house. The Bob and Gale relationship was in danger). He also needed a staff to run the place while he carved. And carved. And carved.

The outside grounds developed pretty much the same way, mostly by happenstance. Gale bought the land across the road. Someone had started to dig a cellar hole there once, but had given up when it filled with water. Bob turned the cellar hole into a pond. Recently, a tree house sprang up beside the museum, thanks to more generous donors and some enthusiastic students at the Essex Center for Technology.

In the summer of 2013, just when the museum collection reached 500 carvings and everything was looking great, a devastating rainstorm hit Huntington and created a gaping chasm where the path from the parking lot used to be. The flood also caused a lot of damage throughout the property. Not long after that, Bob himself passed away at age ninety-four.

Faced with a double tragedy, the people who love the museum never faltered. By 2016, a fine new bridge graced the entrance to the museum, surrounded by carefully chosen native plants. Other carvers are stepping in to fill the void, the staff is creating new programs and exhibits, museum membership is growing, and visitors continue to flock in.

Bob Spear's legacy is big enough to do anyone proud.

# 1
# The Early Years

My chickadee, with friends
*Photo by Kari Jo Spear, 2020*

When I was a little kid, I had no idea my father would one day have his own museum. I didn't even know he carved birds. I just knew that he spent a lot of time down in his den, sitting in an old, brown, leather rocking chair with wide wooden arms, making a huge pile of shavings on the floor in front of him. I loved the shavings. They came in all kinds of interesting shapes. Some were flat; some were twisting. No two were just alike. I would sit on the floor and make jewelry out of them—the long, curly ones made good earrings, and the shorter, curly ones could be hooked together for a bracelet. Some even curled around my fingers for rings. The flat shavings lined up to become roads or fences for my imaginary animals. And if I ever needed one of a certain shape or size, I just had to describe it, and my father would whittle off what I needed. The block of wood in his hands was not remotely interesting, not compared to the ever-growing pile of shavings. If I thought about the block of wood at all, I thought he was carving it up just to make toys for me.

As an adult, I realized that he probably kept a piece of scrap wood handy to oblige me with—surely he wouldn't have been able to always carve off random shapes from the work of art he was in the process of creating.

The den wasn't the only place I could find shavings. My father also carved in the passenger seat of our car during his lunch hour from General Electric in Burlington. This meant the car floor also had a constant covering of shavings, even though my mother insisted that he vacuum it out once in a while. So I had an endless supply of shavings to play with on car rides, though I'm sure my mother wasn't happy with me for getting them all over the seat as well. The first time I rode in a friend's car, I was amazed by the clean floor mats. I thought all cars came with shavings, and I felt sorry for my friend because she didn't have anything to play with.

Eventually, I got old enough to notice that my father was, in fact, making things. He had a birdfeeder right outside the window next to his chair, and I thought it was pretty amazing that he could make blocks of wood turn into the same things that came to the feeder. I learned to recognize chickadees, woodpeckers, and nuthatches. What was amazing was that his birds looked just like the real ones. Their heads were perked up, their feathers were fluffed out, and they even seemed to look at me. Each carving was just a little bit different from the rest and had its own personality.

I liked to watch how the wooden birds came to life when he painted them. One day he let me paint one of the chickadees. It didn't quite look like his when I was finished, but that was okay. I got to keep it when he packed his into a big cardboard box to go to the gift shop where he sold them. And the next day, he'd make more.

My father's carving habit leaked over into the rest of our lives. For instance, whenever we went canoeing, he always watched for interesting pieces of driftwood to mount his carvings on. Sometimes he picked up so much driftwood, there was hardly enough room in the boat for me. I admit I occasionally worried that if he found a perfect piece that was really big, I might get left on the beach.

Then there were the dead birds. My father had a taxidermy license, and he spent many years putting together a collection of specimens to display at the Green Mountain Audubon Center, which he founded after he left General Electric. I know now that his knowledge of how birds work on the inside helped make his carvings so lifelike. But when I was a kid, it meant that our freezer always held dead birds wrapped in tinfoil among the frozen vegetables and ice cream. My mother would want to thaw out a piece of chicken for dinner and get a grosbeak instead. I'd go for a Popsicle and have to rummage through finches.

As a kid, I was as well trained as the best retriever to bring back dead birds. My sharp eyes and nearness to the ground made me invaluable. Once on a trip to Texas, I spotted a man from the motel room next to ours pulling an unfortunate scissor-tailed flycatcher out of the front grille of his car. I saw where he tossed the bird into the bushes. Within moments, I crawled in after it. The car owner was horrified to see a little girl coming out of the shrubbery, raising a dead bird triumphantly and saying it was for her father. I think the fact that my father was absolutely thrilled confused him even more.

Today, that scissor-tailed flycatcher is still mounted in a drawer, my painted chickadee is in my living room, and my father has a whole museum full of his carvings. But as visitors from all over the world walk through the collection, gazing at the spectacular feathering and marveling at the details of the habitat displays, I sometimes catch myself up in the workshop, just running my fingers through a pile of wood shavings.

—*Chip Notes*, Fall 2011

# 2

# Why I'm Not a Carver

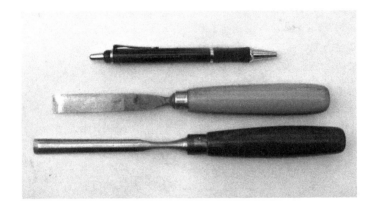

*Photo by Erin Talmage, 2012*

One summer when I was eight or nine years old, my father decided to give carving lessons. About a dozen people signed up, mostly teachers who knew him from the Audubon Society. But three people weren't teachers—my mother, our eleven-year-old neighbor, and me.

We met every Tuesday night in my father's den. It was supposed to be a relaxed, casual gathering of people sitting in a circle, making piles of shavings on the floor while they created things of beauty out of basswood. My father, meanwhile, would circle among them, offering his expert and benign advice. Instead, it turned into a pain-filled bloodbath that caused me so much trauma, I have not even carved a jack-o-lantern since.

And most of it was the fault of the weather.

Vermont is known for crazy weather. That summer was extremely hot and humid. This led to an amazingly regular cycle of thunderstorms that built up all afternoon and let loose in the evening. It seemed that every Tuesday night, the biggest storm of the week unleashed itself. The members of my father's carving class would huddle in the den, away from the windows, and whittle with most of their attention on the wind, rain, and lightning outside. The result was so many nicked thumbs and fingers that my father began bringing Band-Aids to class. There were lots of jokes about everyone carving cardinals and not having to paint them.

I proudly announced that I wanted to carve a horse— I was crazy about birds and horses, and my father already had a monopoly on birds. He dutifully sawed out a block of wood with four legs. My eleven-year-old neighbor was carving a common goldeneye. I don't remember what my mother was making—I'm not sure even she knew. I think she intended to let the wood speak to her.

That night, the worst storm of the summer hit. I glued myself to my mother's side and began to carve. I held the chisel the way my father showed me and carefully pushed it through the wood, aiming away from my fingers. It took a lot of strength, and the end of the chisel looked really, really sharp. I took three gouges out of my horse and stopped, not sure that I wanted to do any more. I really didn't want Band-Aids all over my hands like everybody else. (Except for my father, of course. He was already on his third chickadee for the night.)

Then came a terrible bolt of lightning and a deafening crash of thunder. All the lights in the house went out, and my mother screamed. In the next flash, I saw that her left hand was covered with blood.

My father had a flashlight handy. In its light, he and a couple of my mother's friends whisked her upstairs to the bathroom. I was completely forgotten in the confusion. The next thing I knew, I was sitting with a bunch of mostly strangers in the dark.

I got up to grope my way upstairs, but someone told me to sit still and not move. I was barefoot, and everybody had dropped their tools on the floor. So there I sat, trapped by hostile knives in the worst thunderstorm I could remember, while my mother bled to death upstairs.

Eventually I was remembered, and my father came downstairs to collect me. He was very pale. I remembered that the sight of blood made him squeamish—especially major blood. He distributed flashlights, and we made our way between the carvers as they collected their fallen tools.

In the bathroom, my mother had a towel wrapped around her hand, but she was very much alive and gave me a hug. The wound left her with a scar and some numbness in her thumb, but otherwise she was fine.

At that point, I was having some serious misgivings about my future as a carver. I made my decision the next day, after I walked over to my eleven-year-old neighbor's house. He was sitting on the front steps, wearing shorts, and carving his goldeneye. I called, "Hello!" He looked up, saw me, and buried his chisel to the hilt in his left leg. As his mother rushed him to the ER, I decided that my creativity would have to find another outlet.

Today, my horse with three gouges lies in comfort in my father's cabinet. I think he still hopes I'll get back to it someday. But I know for a fact that the Horses of Vermont Museum will never be. I have decided that pens, while they may be mightier than a sword, are a heck of a lot safer than chisels and knives.

—*Chip Notes*, Winter 2012

# 3
# Something's Going on Here...

My father proudly removing the framework from the
plaster base of the red-winged blackbird display
*Photo by Kari Jo Spear, late 1970s*

My mud
*Photo by Kari Jo Spear, 2020*

I can't remember the first time I ever heard the "M" word. The fact that we were going to have a *museum* in the family emerged very slowly, after a great many permutations and plot twists. By the time it was a reality, it felt like it was meant to be from the beginning. But it didn't start out that way.

Some time after my parents divorced, and when Gale had entered the picture, I began spending a day every weekend with my father. Gale had an old building made of gray cement blocks next to her house. She used it for storage. The foundations of a dismantled barn lay along one side of it. Gale and my father cleaned out the building and put in a woodstove and a workbench. My father moved his tools in, and just like that, he had a workshop. It had a big window with birdfeeders outside. I thought he'd continue making chickadees to sell to gift shops. But I was wrong. He was making "keepers" now.

One late winter day when we walked into the shop, I saw a bunch of cattails standing in the center of the room. The cattails were stuck in a block of pure white plaster. A bird's nest was balanced in the midst of them. My father told me he was going to carve two red-winged blackbirds to perch around the nest. "I want to show the habitat," he explained.

Well, that made sense, except that the habitat was taller than I was.

My father asked, "Do you want to paint the plaster to look like mud?"

Me? Paint the mud?

Like a typical teenager, I searched for the catch. Was this his way of saying he wanted to include me in the project? Obviously, I wasn't going to be doing any of the carving. But was painting mud all I was good for? It also crossed my mind that the height of the cattails would prevent them from being placed atop the workbench, so whoever painted the mud was going to have to do it sitting on the floor.

Well, I decided to take it as an honor, and pretty soon I was sitting with a palette of brown and green paint, happily dabbing away. There is a great variety in the color of mud, especially with some algae mixed in. I threw my heart and soul into making the richest, muddiest mud that cattails ever grew out of.

When I was done, my father looked down at it. "Yup. Looks like mud."

I chose to take it as a compliment.

The next week, there were two red-winged blackbirds mounted to the cattails, the nest had eggs in it, and the whole thing had been enclosed in Plexiglas and was standing in a corner of the shop.

"Going to make the next ones smaller," my father said, nodding to the case. "All that glass is kind of expensive. I'll put them up on wooden bases. Maybe make covers with lights in them."

Okay, that sounded good, I thought. No more sitting on the floor. But I had to say, "Wait, hang on. How many of these are you going to make?"

That's when I saw a glint in my father's eye, and I knew something was brewing. "Well, I don't know. I'd like to do all the birds that nest in Vermont."

I didn't know just how many that was, exactly, but it felt like a lot. "And you're going to make a pair of each of them?"

That little glint got brighter.

Math has never been my thing, but even I could figure out that we were talking hundreds of birds here. In protective cases, with habitats. But the woodshop was the size of, well, a shop, and Gale's house already had, well, house stuff in it.

So I asked the obvious question. "Where are they all going to go?"

There was a moment of silence. Then my father gave his usual response to any difficult question: "Hmm." Which meant, in this case, carve first and worry later.

We went back to contemplating the red-winged blackbirds.

I had no idea what had just begun.

—*Chip Notes*, Spring 2012

# 4

# The Summer of Pies

An assortment of leaves
*Photo by Kari Jo Spear 2020*

One summer day when I was in my early teens, my
father greeted me in the doorway of his shop with two
aluminum pie pans in his hands. He looked really excited.
Since the pie pans were empty, I got a feeling that this had
something to do with the Birds in Their Habitats thing that
he had going.

As soon as I got inside, he asked, "Want to make some leaves?"

He sounded exactly the same way he'd sounded when he'd asked me a few months earlier if I wanted to paint some mud. *Here we go again*, I thought. I was a teenager, and I had, quite frankly, a lot more important things on my mind than birds. Like the novel I was writing, and my friends, and school, and, um, boys. But I knew that no would not be the right answer.

"Okay," I said as unenthusiastically as I could.

Next thing I knew, I was sitting on a stool beside him at his workbench. He handed me a cutting board covered with a thin piece of rubber. What that had to do with leaves, I had no idea. Then I noticed a pile of silvery, oblong shapes on the bench between us. Each one was about three inches long, maybe an inch across, and pointed at the end. They looked like fake fingernails, except they had delicately jagged edges.

"Watch," my father said. He laid down the rubber-covered board, put a fake fingernail on it, and picked up a long, narrow tool like an oversize pencil with a very sharp tip. He pressed the tip gently to one end of the fingernail and drew a fine line straight up the middle to the other end. Then he drew in a lot of little lines running from the center line out to the jagged edges. When he held it up, the fingernail looked like a pretty silver leaf.

"I'll paint it green," he said, as though that would explain everything.

I just looked at him. The word "habitat" formed in my mind. This had to do with habitats, I knew it!

"I've got some more nests," he said, "and the limbs they were built on. But the leaves have all dried up and fallen off. Besides, they have to look like spring if I'm going to carve eggs to go in the nests."

I guessed that made sense. "But how are you going to get the leaves to stick onto the branch?"

"Glue," he said, as though he'd already got it all figured out. "But it's all got to look real, so I'll make some more branches out of wire and wrap them with cotton and coat them with glue. I'll paint them to look like bark, and then glue on more leaves."

I think I might have been staring at him.

"I'll cut the leaves out," he went on as though I was really thrilled about this, "and you can press in the veins. Here." He handed me the sharp tool and pushed the pile of fake fingernails toward me. There were maybe three dozen.

"That's a lot," I said.

He was busy picking up the pie pans and pretended he hadn't heard me—the way people who are hard of hearing are really good at doing. In a minute, he was carefully cutting out more leaves from the bottom of the pan.

I gave in to peer pressure and got to work. My first center vein came out a little crooked, but hey, nature's not perfect. After my fifth leaf, I had the technique down. I was creating some pretty awesome-looking leaves that any nest full of wooden eggs could be proud of.

The problem was that my father was cutting out leaf templates faster than I could press veins into them, so my pile was getting bigger, not smaller. Then he bent down and pulled out a couple more empty pans from beneath the bench.

"Hey, where'd you get all those?" I asked.

He smiled. "Gale's been buying one of every brand she can find. Some pans are a lot better than others. They don't have so much writing and stuff on the bottom, so I've got more space to cut. I think we've got it figured out now."

I just stared at him. Most people bought pies based on how luscious they looked. Gale was buying pies based on what the bottom of the pan looked like?

Then he grinned. "There's a blueberry pie we've got to eat up for lunch."

The day suddenly got a whole lot better.

"Hold on," he said as I was about to jump up. "We've got to get another dozen leaves done first. But there's a cherry pie for dinner."

I gaped at him.

"And maybe you'd like to have some of your friends come up next weekend? I've got plenty of sharp tools. Tell them there'll be lots of pie."

I decided that leaves might be okay after all.

The days became a blur of eating pies and making leaves with my friends and eating more pies. Soon pairs of warblers were perched proudly around nests surrounded by lush green habitats, and I had to buy new clothes because none of the old ones fit any longer.

The glorious summer of pies ended very abruptly one day when the UPS truck pulled up in front of the shop, and a delivery man staggered in. In his arms was the end of an era—a roll of aluminum sheeting the same thickness as a pie pan. It was all shiny and pristine, unmarked by any lettering. It looked like it was five feet long and weighed a couple hundred pounds.

"Gale found it in a catalog and ordered it," my father said very glumly.

I could tell that even he could never make enough leaves to use it all up.

"Oh, well," he said. "There's still a few pies left in the house. Can't let them go to waste, can we?"

We laughed and went back to finish that day's quota of leaves before lunch.

—*Chip Notes*, Fall 2012

# 5
# My Addiction

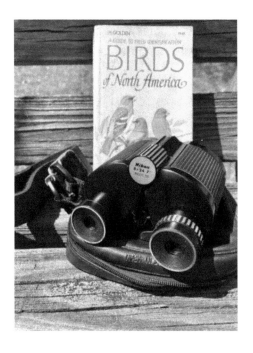

The originals
*Photo by Kari Jo Spear, 2020*

*Addiction*
*a strong inclination to do, use, or indulge in something repeatedly.*
                    *—From Merriam-Webster Online Dictionary*

I sat in my health class, knowing I was doomed. I had all the symptoms: obsession, distraction, longing ... Life as I'd known it was over. And it had all started with a pair of binoculars.

It happened on my eleventh birthday. We were sitting around the kitchen table in Gale's house, and there were two gifts from my father before me. Both were carefully wrapped in the comics pages from the newspaper—he and Gale were recycling and reusing before recycling and reusing were popular. Two innocent packages were about to change my life forever.

Kid fashion, I opened the biggest one first. As the paper fell away, I saw that I held a box containing a brand-new pair of Nikon binoculars.

I looked up. I'd been hoping for books.

"They're the best," my father said excitedly. "Small and light, but with great optics. Eight by twenty-four. That means they magnify eight times larger than you see with the naked eye. Twenty-four is the size of the objective lens. That means they have a superior light-gathering capability."

He must have registered my lack of enthusiasm. "They're what everybody has now," he added.

I was pretty sure none of the kids at school had Nikon 8x24s with superior light-gathering capability. He must mean his birding buddies—folks who wore mud boots, baggy clothes with lots of pockets, and dorky hats. They were always talking about their all-important life lists.

"You'll need this too," my father went on, pushing the other present toward me.

It was a book, but it wasn't fiction. It was *Birds of North America*.

"Wow," I said.

He chose to interpret that as excitement. "Figured you were old enough." He dug my new binoculars out of their Styrofoam packaging as though he was dying to get his hands on them. "This is where you focus."

Like I didn't know what the knob in the middle was for. I'd played with his binoculars when I was younger. I liked looking through a lens backward—it made everything seem really far away. My father carried binoculars wherever he went. I'd never seem him use them when he was actually driving, but I wouldn't have put it past him if something he needed for his life list flew over.

He was waiting for me to do the obvious, so I picked them up. *Well*, I thought, *this isn't the end of the world.* I got dragged on bird walks all the time. It would be good not to have to stand around getting cold or swatting bugs, pretending I could see what everybody was so excited about. At least the binoculars were light, so my neck wouldn't break.

I raised them and turned to the window, where a bunch of chickadees swarmed like bees around a feeder. I looked, focused, and—*holy cow*! I could see their eyeballs! All the little feathers on their heads stood out. Their sharp beaks dug into seeds they anchored with their feet.

My father chuckled. I lowered my binoculars quickly. Ten minutes had gone by. Huh.

Then my father pushed the bird book toward me. "This is where you mark your life list," he said, pointing out pages and pages of bird names in the back. Each name had a little box to tick in front of it.

Like I was going to start a life list. The kids at school would never let me live it down. Not that any of them knew what a life list was.

"You've already got a bigger one than a lot of people," my father said, tapping his finger partway down a page. "Start here. You've seen common loons when we've been canoeing."

"You mean, I can count species I've already seen?"

"Sure." He handed me a pen.

Dutifully, I ticked the box next to common loon. "Hey, can I count the red-throated loon we saw on the ocean?" I recalled him dragging my attention away from the lovely sailboats for that.

"Of course."

I filled in that one too, and flipped back a few pages. "I've seen lots of gulls."

"Ah, but were they ring-billed or herring?"

I didn't know gulls came in different flavors. According to the book, there were at least half a dozen in Vermont regularly!

"Burger King parking lot," my father said. "We'll eat there tonight and you'll be able to see them close enough to tell them apart."

Well, I wasn't going to say no to French fries.

"And look! There are sparrows under the lilac. You can get two—no, *three* species right now!"

I had my binoculars up before I even realized it. When I looked down a few minutes later, my father had my book open to the sparrow section. He had a grin on his face.

It began gently, but the addiction had taken a firm hold already. I knew it was too late.

—*Chip Notes*, Winter 2013

# 6

# Habitat Shots

A typical habitat shot
*Photo by Kari Jo Spear, 2020*

"Take a shot in that direction." My father pointed down toward the brook through some hemlock trees. "Good ruffed grouse territory."

"Okay," I said.

My job was to take an interesting photo. So I crouched down, trying to get into ruffed grouse mode, going for an eye-level perspective. If I were a grouse, I'd lay my eggs right under the trees.

Of course, I wasn't a grouse, and this was another of my father's crazy attempts to get me into his "carve all the birds in Vermont" project. He thought it would be helpful to have a plastic sleeve hanging from each display case with some facts about the bird and a photo of its nesting habitat. I thought all the leaves and flowers and stuff he was putting in the cases would be enough to clue people in, but he wanted photos too. Wouldn't it be nice if I took them?

Well, I liked taking photos, and my father's fancy Nikon with interchangeable lenses made me look like a young, serious photographer. But nesting habitat was not exactly an exciting subject to photograph. We'd been hiking for hours, and I'd dutifully taken shots of deciduous trees, evergreens, moss, and even dead stumps.

That part wasn't so bad, though. The real problem was that habitat shots had to be taken in the spring, when the birds were nesting. The birds nested then to take advantage of their favorite food source—insects, who were also doing their multiplying thing. And right then, every black fly in Huntington was taking advantage of *their* favorite food source—me. They didn't care about my artistic endeavor. They didn't care that I reeked of insect repellant. They didn't care that I was allergic to them. My eyes were going to be puffed shut the next day, I knew it.

*I am a grouse,* I thought. I snapped two more shots down toward the brook, even climbing into the brush to get a nice, curving limb to frame the top.

"Okay," my father said. "Now I want to go to a farm up the road. There's a pair of cliff swallows building under the eaves of the barn. We can get barn swallow habitat inside. And all the apple trees are in bloom. They're real pretty, and they'd be good bluebird habitat."

Anything to get away from the buggy brook. I swatted my way out of the woods—flies never seemed to bother my father—and scratched my way up the road to an old farm that looked as though it had been there since the glaciers moved out. I liked the way the buildings nestled into the hillside.

Sure enough, there was a small colony of cliff swallows building their funny little jug-like nests under the eaves. I didn't even ask how my father had known they were there. While he chatted with the farmer, I photographed the eaves and some rafters inside, where the barn swallows were busy irritating the cows. Then I wandered around the apple trees in full bloom and thought about how nice a big bee sting would look right between my puffy eyes. Maybe some poison ivy to set it off.

In the middle of these self-pitying daydreams, I tripped over a branch buried in the new spring grass and landed in a woodchuck hole, twisting my ankle.

My father got the car and drove me home. Fortunately, I wasn't bleeding—"Not as bad as the carving classes," he pointed out. And the camera was okay, so there was no harm done.

"An old warhorse," he said, looking at the camera on the seat between us. I didn't think he was referring to me. I was a young warhorse, maybe. "You may as well keep it."

"Until next weekend?" I asked, wondering if my ankle would be up to more traipsing around.

He kind of shrugged. "Till whenever. If I need it for something, you can bring it back."

"Oh," I said as it slowly sank in that he'd just given me a really nice camera. On a kind of permanent borrow.

"Might as well take the lenses too."

I noticed that they were in the backseat. A 300 mm lens and a wide-angle. "Thanks," I said, meaning it.

"It's a good camera," he said.

And that was that.

Then he added, "But we need to get the film developed right away."

"What's the rush?"

"Montpelier."

*O-kaay*, I thought. Montpelier is Vermont's state capital.

"Library," he added.

"You're going to carve books next?" I'd believe anything.

He shot me a look. "No. Going to have the carvings there next week."

"*What?*"

"There's an art gallery upstairs in the library," he said patiently. "We're going to have a big opening. Newspapers will be there."

I looked at him. At least he hadn't said he was running for governor. But how had he known how to set up something like that? He'd probably enlisted Gale. He didn't even look nervous. I'd have been frantic.

---

"We've got to start getting people interested in the project, you know," he went on. "Need to find someplace to house them."

"Them" meant the carvings, and he was right. At the rate he was going, he wouldn't have room to breathe in the shop much longer.

"There'll be a reception. With food." He looked at me hopefully.

"Of course I'll be there," I said. And not just for the food.

"Good." He smiled, just a little. "It's upstairs. Your ankle will be better by next weekend, right?"

Of course it would be. Who wouldn't want to get all hot and sweaty lugging bird cases to an upstairs gallery? I heaved a sigh. I'd never figure out how he managed to talk me into getting deeper and deeper into this project of his.

The next morning, I limped into school with my eyes puffed mostly shut, my arms and legs sunburned and dotted with red spots, and my left ankle wrapped up.

"What happened to you?" my homeroom teacher asked.

All around us were kids with honorable injuries, acquired by heroically sliding into home plate or bursting across a finish line. Everyone turned to me, waiting to hear my glorious tale.

I dropped into my desk with a sigh. "Woodchuck hole."

Everyone's eyebrows went up.

I nodded wisely, like this was a big deal. Lowering my voice, I said, "Okay. Let me tell you guys about ... habitat shots."

*Author's Note*: Visitors to the museum will notice there are no photographs hanging from any of the cases. My father finally realized—as *someone* had tried to tell him—that people would get the idea where the birds nested from all the leaves and flowers and stuff in the cases. The habitat-photography phase passed quickly. But to this day, if I take a photo with no apparent subject, my father will look at it, smile a little, and say, "Looks like a habitat shot to me."

And I still have the camera, tucked away somewhere safe. Permanent borrow: thirty-five years and counting.

—*Chip Notes*, Spring 2013

# 7

# How You Know When You're Growing Up

My father at the door of the shop.
Notice the little bit of foundation on the left showing
where the addition will later stand.
*Photo by Kari Jo Spear, late 1970s*

Things were starting to get out of hand.

My father's carvings had been well received during their debut in the art gallery in Montpelier. People had flocked to see them. Photos had been taken. Articles had been written. In short, Vermont was interested in his project. After their few weeks of fame and glory, the carvings were returned to my father's shop in triumph.

The problem was, they seemed to have grown while they'd been gone. Or else the shop had shrunk. The first day they were back, I stood in the doorway, surveying the long, rectangular room. Or trying to survey it. I couldn't really see it—or the workbench, or the woodstove, or any of my father's tools. Or my father, for that matter, and even in his younger days, he was hard to miss. (Meaning that he wore red shirts back then too, of course! I'm not implying *anything* about his, er, generally recognizable shape.) The whole room was full, as far as I could tell, of leafy branches, tree trunks, and bright spots of plumage.

"I'm back here!"

My father's voice came from somewhere near the window. I turned sideways and squeezed between Plexiglas cases in his direction, stopping to glance at my favorites: the red-winged blackbirds. Yup, the mud I'd painted still looked good.

I finally found my father sitting on his stool, peering my way. "You made it," he said.

"Yeah. It's getting a little tight in here. What'd they feed these guys in Montpelier, anyway? Did they put steroids in the suet or something?"

My father didn't laugh. "I've been talking to the Shelburne Farms people. And the Ethan Allen Homestead people."

"About?" I prompted.

"Housing them," he said. "The collection."

So he'd evidently noticed the overcrowding of the avian population, too.

"Were they interested?" As tight as it was getting in there, I suddenly felt kind of funny about the carvings going away permanently. I'd missed them while they were off on their maiden flight. Would strangers take good care of my mud and everything? I mean, that mud was the first and only mud I'd ever painted! It wasn't just any mud. It was part of my childhood memories.

"No one seems to think they've got enough room."

"Are you kidding me? Those barns at Shelburne Farms are huge!"

My father cleared his throat and said something that sounded like "... more cases, and a wetland diorama, and endangered species."

I blinked. "You mean, there's going to be a lot more? A *lot* more?"

My father looked kind of sheepish and muttered about investors and interested parties. I didn't know much about that kind of thing, but I knew that he was talking about money. For the first time, I began to realize that this project might get really, really big. And not only that, it might really happen.

"Holy cow," I said. "Are you, like, going to get famous?"

My father suddenly looked horrified and leaped off his stool. "Let's go canoeing," he said in a rush, and he was gone as though he'd grown wings himself.

It took me a lot longer to find my way to the door of the shop. Something in the atmosphere had suddenly changed. I looked at the cases and the birds inside them in a new way. Yeah, they were bigger all right. Even my mud didn't feel as though it was all mine any longer. Whatever was happening here might get really weird—like, turn into a legacy or something. It could outlast my father.

And even me.

—*Chip Notes*, Winter 2014

# 8
# My Dead Arm

My father and Gale celebrating
the opening of the museum
*Photographer unknown, 1987*

My arm was killing me. My muscles burned, my fingers cramped, and my shoulder barely fit in its socket any longer. In other words, I was in agony, and it was all my father's fault. I was furious with those stupid birds of his and his stupid idea about carving every freaking bird that had ever been stupid enough to set its freaking feathers in Vermont. I was even madder about his stupid idea to rebuild the barn on the old foundation next to Gale's house and keep his stupid birds in there.

I was going to be maimed for life because of this! I was never going to be able to use my right arm again. My fingers were ice cold and I could barely feel them, much less move them. Any doctor would agree this was child abuse. I should be put into foster care and live in a nice, normal apartment in a city and never have to look at another bird as long as I lived!

Not only that, but my hand was sticky, and I hated that more than anything.

I forced my smile back on. "And what would you like?" I asked a sweet little girl standing in front of me.

"Chocolate, please," she said with an eager light in her eyes.

"Chocolate it is, then," I said, and bent over the cooler again, trying to hide my pain.

I had been scooping ice cream for three hours. It had seemed like a really good idea at first. My father was hosting his first open house. It had been advertised all across the media. His "project," now officially called the Birds of Vermont Museum, was open for visitors. In reality, today's open house was a test to see if anybody was interested. To see if anybody was insane enough to drive all the way out to Huntington to look at a bunch of wooden birds. Of course, there was no charge. We were still ages away from having the permits and stuff that were required to become a business, even one that was not for profit.

To sweeten the deal, my father was offering a free dish of Ben and Jerry's ice cream to everybody who showed up that day. For some stupid reason, the ice cream gurus had donated a bunch of bottomless cardboard tubs of the rock hard, icy, sticky stuff for the occasion. And for some stupid reason, I'd thought that was really nice of them and volunteered to be in charge of it.

Now my right arm was totally dead. I hadn't thought that anything could ever make me hate chocolate. But that afternoon was doing a good job of it.

"Here you go." I handed the little girl her dish and dragged my eyes to her mom. "And for you?"

"Vanilla, please," she said.

I decided to hate vanilla too. I made my poor, abused fingers close around the scoop that lived in the vanilla tub.

"And how were you lucky enough to rate this job?" the mom asked.

I looked up at her as though she were out of her freaking mind. Beyond her, the line of people reached across Gale's kitchen, down the hall, out the front door, along the path, over the driveway, and beside the road all the way to the workshop. Which we were now supposed to call the Freaking Birds of Vermont Museum.

"I'm his daughter," I growled.

"Oh, how marvelous! Your father has such incredible talent! Such patience! Such vision!"

I sent her another glance to see if she was sane.

"To create such a project! And not want to make any money at it! All that work to educate people about nature and conservation and—oh, everything! I had to come up here the minute I heard about it. This is something that must happen. I wanted my daughter to be able to say she saw it in its earliest days." She nodded at the little girl dripping chocolate all over the place, who nodded back vigorously. Then the mom smiled at me. "You are so lucky to be part of all this."

My arm suddenly felt a little less leaden and sticky. Did she really mean she hadn't come all this way for free Ben and Jerry's?

"I mean, look at the turnout!" she said. "There are hundreds of people here. You must be so proud."

"It's amazing," someone behind her said.

"They look alive," someone else said.

"I'm going to start a life list," another voice added.

*No, don't!* I almost said aloud. *It won't lead to good things!* But I found myself really smiling as I handed the mom her little dish. "Here you go," I said. "Thanks much for visiting the Birds of Vermont Museum today. And what kind would you like, sir?" I asked the next person in line. "We have chocolate and vanilla and suet with sunflower sprinkles. Just kidding."

He laughed. "Chocolate, please."

"Coming right up. Don't let it drip on your binoculars."

Everyone laughed. *What great people*, I thought. *What a momentous day!*

*And what big muscles I'm going to have.*

—*Chip Notes*, Summer 2014

# 9

# Canoe Lessons

My father was always happy when he
was getting ready to go canoeing
*Photo by Kari Jo Spear, mid 1970s*

In one thing, my father and I were always in perfect
accord. He may have dragged me kicking and screaming
into the world of birding, but I always loved to canoe.
From the time I was old enough to reach over the gunwale,
I had a paddle in my hands. My first one was a blue plastic

badminton racquet attached to a thwart with a string. I paddled my little heart out with it, stirring up white water with my back-and-forth motions and getting soaking wet while my father paddled serenely along in the stern. I always wondered why everybody laughed when they saw us coming.

When I was old enough to graduate to a wooden paddle, my father had me sit in the bow. I'd hardly learned the basic strokes when he put me in the stern and took the bow himself.

"Wait, this is where you steer from," I said.

"Yeah," he said and demonstrated the J-stroke for me.

Surprisingly, it was really easy to make the canoe go where I wanted it to, unlike riding a bike or doing math. My father preferred to hug the shoreline. Watching for shorebirds wasn't enough for him—he wanted to see warblers too. I ran him into a few low-hanging limbs at first, but he didn't mind, even when spiders fell onto his head. (They always seemed to find their way along the length of the canoe to my bare toes.) Soon he began giving me complex directions, like "Bring us in sideways next to that log. Back up a little. Hold it right there." It took me a while to notice he wasn't paddling—he was looking through his binoculars into the trees. Huh.

Once I got really good at steering, he taught me how to paddle without taking the paddle out of the water. "It's the way the Indians used to do it," he said. "You don't make any noise at all. Take a regular stroke and then sort of glide the paddle up ahead of you through the water, angled a little. That's it."

My paddle slid through the water like a silent knife, completely eliminating the plunk of the blade breaking the surface and the silvery rain of drops coming off the edge when it swept forward. I imagined Indians sneaking up on their enemies, soundless in the night.

"Works great to get close to a heron," my father said.

That too.

The first time I ever paddled solo was on a field trip, and my being alone in the canoe wasn't planned. There were seven or eight canoes in our group, and we spent the day making our way down Otter Creek in Vergennes, Vermont. Early that morning, we had left a car in a pull-off near where we planned to end our trip so that the drivers of the other cars could ride back in it to where we'd started. That way we wouldn't have to paddle back upstream against the current.

By late afternoon, everyone was tired, hot, hungry, sunburned, bug bitten, sick of sitting, and in urgent need of a pee (at least, I was). But we couldn't find the pull-off where we'd left the car that morning. From the level of the creek, it was impossible to see the road, due to the height of the banks.

A discussion broke out over whether we'd passed the car or if it was still ahead. My father told everybody to rest in the shade, and he'd go on downstream a ways. Since I was paddling with him, that meant I was going on too. So we kept going.

And going.

And going.

My father didn't usually get lost (except in the mall), and pretty soon he was frowning. At last, he told me to land us on a tiny strip of sand. He said that he'd walk across a field, find the road, and look around for the car. It had to be somewhere nearby.

As soon as we were beached, he took off—and I peed. Then I waited alone by the canoe for about fifteen minutes. At last, I heard him shout from a long distance farther down the creek: he'd found the car.

Yay.

To save time, he instructed, I should paddle back and get the others.

Not so yay.

But I yelled back that I would. The canoe seemed to get a whole lot bigger and heavier, and kind of scary. He'd once told me the best place to paddle solo was kneeling in the center with the boat facing the other way around, going stern first. That would keep the canoe level. So I climbed into the center, knelt down, rested my butt on the edge of a thwart, and pushed off. I felt like I was paddling through molasses, until I remembered I was going against the current. Not to mention I was dead tired. But I was used to being the only one paddling a good deal of the time while my father was birding, so soon I had some momentum going. I kept close to shore. After a while, my heart rate settled down.

At long last, the other canoes came into sight, nosed into shore. A collection of people who looked like shipwreck survivors were collapsed in the shade. They saw me coming, and someone shouted, "Oh my God, where's your father?" They jumped up like they thought he'd fallen overboard and had been eaten by a giant snapping turtle.

I yelled back, "He walked to the car! He says to keep coming."

As they piled back into their canoes, someone asked if I wanted a bow paddler. I shook my head, turned the canoe on a dime, and paddled Indian-style back downstream.

Yeah, canoeing was my thing, for sure.

—*Chip Notes*, Winter 2015

# 10

# Battlefields

My father and a Revolutionary War cannon
at Fort Ticonderoga, New York
*Photo by Ingrid Rhind, 2006*

If birds were my father's first passion, the Civil War was his second. (Family, he pretty much took for granted.) He could fight every battle from memory, including all the skirmishes leading up to it as well as the aftermath. He could discuss the finer points of each battle's contribution to the war and its enduring legacies. He focused on Vermonters, especially his great-grandfather and hero, Alonzo Spear. Yet he always held Robert E. Lee in the highest regard.

For a long time, I couldn't understand why my peace-loving, crowd-hating, and squeamish father was so fascinated by battlefields. When I asked him, all he would say was "Well, they're kind of interesting."

One day, my father, Gale, and I visited Hubbardton Battlefield, where Vermont's only Revolutionary War battle took place. None of us had ever been there before. In the visitor center was a diorama depicting the movements of the troops during the engagement. I stood in front of it, feeling baffled.

My father silently contemplated the scenario for a few moments and then launched into a full explanation. He waved his hands over the diorama like a conductor, commenting on the initial positions of both sides, the strategic fallbacks, the flanking attempts, and the outcome. (We lost. But we Vermonters achieved our goal of halting the British in their tracks long enough to allow the main American force to get away. See, I was listening.)

Unbeknownst to us, a member of the staff had been listening too. "You must be a scholar of this aspect of the Revolution," he said to my father.

My father shook his head. "Not really. But it's kind of interesting."

When we got outside, I said, "I thought you'd never been here before."

"I haven't. But these battles are really simple compared to the Civil War." In other words, he'd figured the whole thing out in about a minute.

My father really was a scholar of the Civil War. I don't think there is any book, article, or movie he hasn't memorized. About the only reason he'd leave our museum for a vacation was to tour a battlefield. He visited all the major ones, figuring out exactly where Alonzo would have been standing. Poor Gale would often say with a sigh, "We're off to fight the Civil War again." So much for tropical beaches.

After the internet came into being, I sometimes researched the 2nd Vermont Regiment. When I watched the documentaries, I tried to figure out where my great-great grandfather had been standing. (Alonzo had been in the thick of things at Gettysburg, one of the heroic Vermonters who saved the day and perhaps even turned the tide of the war.) I read and watched more. It was addictive. And ancestral.

I imagined what my father would have been like if he'd lived back then. General Spear. It would have been … interesting.

—*Chip Notes*, Summer 2016

# 11

# My Father and the Speedboat

The site of the famous disaster on
Malletts Bay, Lake Champlain
*Photo by Kari Jo Spear, 2016*

One family story from before I was born has haunted
me. I could never get my head around the fact that my
quiet, slow-moving father had once owned a speedboat and
raced around Lake Champlain in it. Why he no longer

owned it had been obscured by the mists of time before I was old enough to ask questions.

All my father would say was "I hit a rock." End of discussion. End, I assumed, of the speedboat. This helped explain why my father never had anything good to say about the smelly, gas-wasting, pollution-causing noisemakers that went so fast you couldn't tell the difference between ring-billed and herring gulls as you roared by.

My mother didn't like to talk about the boat either, but her version was more detailed than his. According to her, the rock incident happened one summer evening in Malletts Bay, near my family's camp. She, my father, my uncle, my grandmother, and one of my great-aunts were out in the boat, enjoying the sunset. The 1950s-style boat was made of dark wood and had two bench seats running across the middle. The steering wheel was in the front. My father was operating it—fast.

Suddenly, according to my mother, there was a jolt. The boat's speed and direction didn't change. The boat just no longer had a bottom. She could see the water rushing below her feet, as if the floor had been peeled away by a giant can opener. She said my father looked down and killed the engine—and the boat promptly sank.

Yup, hit a rock.

Fortunately, no one was hurt. Another boater rescued them from the water as it was getting dark and returned them, tired and wet, to our family camp. Waiting relatives had become frantic, knowing that something had happened, but not what.

Recently, I emailed my uncle, who now lives in Nevada, to see what he remembered about the incident. He gave me the most detailed account I've yet heard about what he called "The Great Boat Wreck Caper." He described a late afternoon ride along the shore in the family's new boat. They had slowed down to look at trees and cliffs. (I suspect there might have been cliff swallows too, but that's just speculation.) Then, "Bob, who was driving, picked up speed, and as we hit full speed, we also hit a submerged rock or ledge. After a few seconds of bewilderment, we looked down and saw water pouring into the boat through a large gash in the bottom. It quickly became evident that we couldn't stay in the boat, so we abandoned ship." The boat sank stern-first, looking "exactly like pictures of ships that have been torpedoed."

But here my uncle's version is more detailed than those my parents told. The boat didn't go straight to the bottom. The bow remained floating just above the surface. And the survivors weren't picked up immediately by a rescue boat. They swam back to and stood on the guilty iceberg—er, rock, while someone on shore launched another boat and came out to them. (I am sorely tempted to make a comment about a flock of gulls vying for standing room, but I won't.) After the rescue boat arrived and they were safely aboard, the rescuer towed the disabled boat to the nearest beach, where my father and my uncle removed the motor. Then the rescuer returned the bedraggled survivors, with motor, to camp. My uncle stayed up late that night, disassembling the motor and drying it.

My uncle went on, "The next morning, Bob woke me up early so we could take his canoe back to where we had beached the boat. We hooked a line to it and towed it back to camp." (I sense this might have been the moment when the canoe rose to the top of my father's list of worthwhile boats.) My father and my uncle went back, again by canoe, to the site of the disaster, where they dived for loose articles that had fallen out of the doomed boat—including my uncle's wallet. (Yes, he found it, along with his car keys, still in the pocket of a pair of pants he'd thrown in the boat at the last minute.)

My uncle finished, "Over the next few days, Bob worked out that we could screw a plywood patch into the hole in the bottom and cover it with fiberglass. It didn't look great but it worked fine, so we were back in business." (Add speedboat repair to my father's résumé.) Still, I infer that the family's interest in speedboats had ebbed, and my uncle said the boat was sold a few years later.

Though my father didn't talk about that day much, I remember him pointing to a marker on the map of the lake that hangs on the camp wall. The mark denoted a dangerous shallow spot in the middle of otherwise deep water. My father smiled a little and said, "Yep, I found that one."

Like my father, I have chosen quiet, reflective paddling over speed. A few weeks ago, I paddled my trusty kayak deeper into Malletts Bay than I'd ever gone before. The lake level was at a near record low. As I came around a point of land, I saw a dark ledge of rock breaking the surface. Next to it was a white buoy with "DANGER" in red on the side. And I realized what I must be looking at.

The infamous rock ledge that had torpedoed my father's boat was actually above the surface for the first time in years.

I paddled around it and photographed it with my cell phone. Then I just drifted a while, listening to the gurgle of water and the cries of gulls, and looked deep into the reflections on the water's surface.

—*Chip Notes*, Fall 2016

# 12

## Daughter vs. Tractor

My father's tractor
*Photo by Erin Talmage, 2017*

I had never been so terrified in my life.

I usually loved sugaring season. Maple permeated my life for those short, intense weeks between winter and spring. I loved the trees as they came to life, loved how the spring whistles of chickadees answered the gentle creak of my father's hand awl as he tapped the trees. I loved the first pinging of sap into metal buckets, loved the smell of the steam-filled sugar house, and loved the quiet roar of the evaporator over a crackling wood fire. I even loved helping out at the famous sugar-on-snow parties at the Audubon Nature Center, endlessly explaining to visitors the route that a drop of sap took on its adventure from tree to metal can.

But I did *not* like the nature center's tractor.

It was a red behemoth with rear tires that were taller than I was. It had a seat on a spring that bounced up and down, and a little pipe on the top where exhaust came out. I liked riding on the back of it just fine, standing behind my father and holding on to his shoulders. I also liked standing on the wooden runner boards of the gathering tank while my father towed it among the trees. It was especially fun when my father drove through the muddy brook and the water gushed over the boards. I had to pick my feet up and cling to the tank itself. He would always glance over his shoulder to make sure I hadn't been swept downstream.

But the tractor itself was loud and scary.

One year on the first day of tapping, when I was about twelve, my father hitched the tractor to the wooden flatbed trailer and loaded up with hundreds of stacked buckets. The routine was that he would drive through the orchard, stopping at central locations, and we would carefully place the required number of buckets at the base of each maple. Then, over the next few days, he and volunteers would tap the trees and hang the buckets.

But he was the one who made the all-important decision about how many buckets each tree should have. The decision was based mostly on the size of the tree—the older, larger trees got more, trees smaller than a certain circumference got none. Few trees ended up with more than three buckets, spaced well apart. Some people who were tapping trees needed to measure them first, but my father could just look at a tree and know from instinct. Considering he had been tapping the same maples for years, he probably could remember how many buckets each tree got. I always got the feeling, as he moved quietly among them, that they were old friends of his. I suspected that when he was alone, he talked to the trees, and I was also pretty sure they talked back.

Before we headed out that morning, he paused. "If someone drove the tractor slowly," he said, looking right at me, "and I walked along beside it to scatter buckets, this wouldn't take so long."

Behind me, I felt the tractor getting taller by the second.

"You do know I'm twelve, right?" I asked. "And I can't get my learner's permit for three more years?"

My father did that shrugging thing he did. He'd grown up on a farm and had been driving tractors since he was six, the way most farm kids did. I hadn't grown up on a farm. I think he forgot that sometimes.

"Well, you've got long legs," he said. "I'll show you how."

Before I agreed, he swung himself up onto the seat. I climbed to my spot behind him. He fired up the engine and pushed on pedals I'd never noticed before. He did something else with his right hand on little sticky-up things near the steering wheel. All the time, he was talking very loudly over his shoulder at me.

I found myself nodding. It was kind of like when he explained my math homework. I understood it as he went, but by the time he got to the last step, the first few were long gone from my brain.

After a little while, he stopped. "Okay?" he asked.

"Yeah, I don't know," I said.

He took that as an affirmative, and we traded spots.

Yes, the tractor was at least six times taller when I was in the bouncy seat.

"See, your feet reach," he said from where he stood at my shoulder.

I looked ahead. We were on the side of a hill. The road was just a little wider than the tractor, and it was sunk between banks. Innocent maples grew close. I glanced over my shoulder. The trailer loaded with buckets was wider than the tractor.

"Stop before you get to the brook," my father said. "You probably don't want to try that today."

I shot him an incredulous glance, but he was already telling me what to do with my feet and the little sticky-up things. I drew a deep breath, held it, and tapped the thing he'd called a clutch very gently with the toe of my boot.

"Clomp on it," he said.

I clomped.

Things happened fast. The red behemoth made a deeper-throated growl than I'd ever heard. A huge puff of dark smoke came out of the pipe. There was a lurch and a jolt, and we blasted forward.

My normally unflappable father yelled something that sounded like "Steer!" But the wind racing past me tore his words away. I looked up from my feet at the road, but it was gone. There wasn't anything except maples in front of us.

I heard the word "Brake!" but I had no clue which pedal that was. The maples were picking up speed. So I slammed both my feet down on everything they could reach.

With the shriek of overstressed metal, the tractor jerked to a halt and shut itself off, tilted to one side. Behind me, piles of neatly stacked buckets toppled into each other, flew off the trailer, crashed to the ground, and rolled down the hill.

For a while, my father and I were silent, listening to buckets slam into trees. Then it was very quiet.

"Huh," I said.

"Well," my father said. "Guess that's one way to scatter buckets."

He kind of laughed, but I wasn't feeling it. He jumped down and had to give me a hand, because my knees weren't working any longer.

The tires on one side of the tractor were in the road and the other side was up on the bank. There was a maple about five inches in front of the grille. I thought the poor tree looked kind of pale. If it had had apples, I'm sure it would have thrown some at me.

"Did I kill it?" I asked, nodding at the tractor.

My father snorted. "It's a Farmall."

Still, I noticed he gave it an apologetic pat as he climbed up to the seat. While he backed onto the road, I started picking up buckets.

Hours later, when it was getting dark, we walked to the parking lot. Before we got into the car, my father stopped and looked at me. "Three years, you said?"

"Maybe longer," I said.

He nodded fervently.

—*Chip Notes*, Summer 2017

# 13

# Lost in the Bog

A bog with a boardwalk in the
Silvio O. Conte National Wildlife Refuge
*Photo by Dennis Lanpher, 2019*

I'd always thought that bogs were kind of cool. They had neat plants that ate prey alive, and I'd read that if you fell in, your body would be preserved and turn up in a thousand years or so when somebody was cutting peat moss. If you jumped on it, what looked like solid ground would ripple away from you as though you were dancing on the surface of water.

The best part was that bogs—or at least the ones I knew—had lovely boardwalks winding through them. No scrambling over rocks or roots and getting hot and dirty, which were the main reasons I didn't much enjoy hiking. So when my father asked if I wanted to go on a field trip he was leading into a bog, I said sure. I should have been tipped off when he said to wear old sneakers or boots.

About a dozen of us arrived at the designated parking place early in the morning on a lovely, sunny day in May. Except that the moment we got out of the cars, the wind whipped up, the temperature dropped twenty degrees, and it began to rain. None of us had raincoats. I knew that wasn't going to stop my father, so I pulled up the hood of my sweatshirt and prepared to make the best of it. Hopefully any self-respecting bird would go for cover on a day like this. I figured that, after a quick and fruitless stroll along a boardwalk, we'd be heading for a nice dry restaurant to have lunch.

I looked for the trailhead. All I could see was a cow pasture. My father happily climbed through the fence, and the rest of the group trooped after him. *Okay*, I thought, *maybe he told me to wear old sneakers in case I step in some cow mementoes before we get to the boardwalk*. I climbed through the fence too, and had no trouble avoiding the evidence that this was, in fact, a field on an active farm.

We walked down a steep hill to what appeared through the mist to be a swamp at the bottom of the valley. "Here we are," my father said brightly, pointing to rotting logs, dead trees festooned with hanging moss, and pools of water choked with duckweed. "It's right out there."

The mist turned into thick fog, and the rain picked up. I peered around for the elusive boardwalk. *It must be the world's narrowest one*, I thought. Then I got a sinking feeling. "What's right out there?" I asked.

"The bog," my father said, a little slowly, as though I really should have remembered why we were here. "It starts on the other side of this swampy area."

I abruptly noticed that everyone was tucking their pants into their boots. With no further ado, my father set off through the duckweed, clambering over rotting logs and pushing past moss-festooned trees. I bit back a groan as we followed him in.

At first, we tried to pick out a pathway, keeping to what passed for higher ground. But the footing grew wetter, squishier, and muddier. People in boots looked with sympathy at my sneakers—at first. Soon enough they were in over their boot tops and had to stop, sit on a log, and dump out slimy water. I had the better deal with lighter footwear. I tried to pretend I was a swamp sprite, gracefully leaping from bough to hillock. But soon I too was feeling waterlogged. Very waterlogged. The rain had turned to a downpour. And the wind was colder.

"Here's peat moss!" my father suddenly exclaimed.

Sure enough, the stuff we were walking on—it hadn't been "ground" for a long while—turned into a densely woven mat of peat that stretched in all directions as far as the eye could see. That wasn't saying much at that moment, of course. Nevertheless, we all got excited and jumped up and down and laughed at the ripples we made.

They were definitely bigger than the ripples caused by walking on a boardwalk.

Once we'd all had fun rippling, and no one had seen a single bird, I was more than ready for a restaurant. Unfortunately, lunch turned out to be granola bars munched as we walked, or rather squished, farther and farther into the bog. We saw pitcher plants and bog cotton and cute miniature trees that looked like wild bonsai. My father finally spotted a couple miserable-looking cedar waxwings. A crow cawed in the distance. But what we mostly saw was lots and lots of fog. The air got colder and colder.

My father cautioned us to stay away from black spots, where the peat was rotten and a person could fall through. Almost at once, we came to one—an ominous circle of black moss and dark water. "I didn't mean it about the thousand-year-old bodies," I whispered, and kept repeating it as the air grew even colder.

Someone found a spot where methane gas was leaking to the surface—from one of the bodies, I figured. He lit it on fire with his lighter. Flames shot into the sky with a whoosh and then went out. I heard the voice of Gollum in my head, telling me not to follow the lights. I spied the hilts of swords from a long-forgotten battle poking through the moss. Dragons moved sinuously through the fog. Then it got too dim to see much of anything.

I wasn't the only one glad to hear a warm, welcoming moo in the distance. We all flocked toward the sound. Soon we were wallowing through the swamp again, this time not even trying to stay clean. Then we were on solid ground—ground!— and at last we climbed back through the fence and stood on the edge of the road.

There were no parked cars in sight.

"Well, I'll be," my father said. "I think we got turned around in the fog and we've come out on the other side of the valley." He glanced back.

"Yeah, no," I said before he could even suggest going through the bog again. All the moss would look black now.

On the other hand, it could be miles to walk to the cars.

"Okay," my father said. He stepped confidently to the edge of the road and raised his thumb.

I had never seen my father hitchhike in my life. Nor could I imagine anyone stopping for a bunch of bog wraiths. Not that there would be any cars on this forsaken stretch of road anyway.

Suddenly a dragon with fiery eyes swooped out of the dark. To my amazement, it stopped before my father, probably thinking he was a Celtic god of old, or an ancient heroic statue come to life. I heard my father saying something about birding in the bog and the fog, and the next thing I knew, he and several other people were getting on board the dragon and flying off.

The rest of us wraiths sank onto the grass beside the road. Someone said, "I think we're a little hypothermic."

I thought so, too. It was confirmed in a few minutes, because a whole flock of dragons with glowing eyes arrived and swept us off to a place that a had a fire and hot cider. A little while later, I was in a wonderfully warm shower, and then in my very own clean and dry bed.

The last thing I heard before I fell asleep was Doc Brown, or maybe it was my father, saying, "Boardwalks? Where we're going, we don't need boardwalks!"

The swamp sprite in me smiled and agreed.

—*Chip Notes*, Fall 2017

# 14

# My Father the Activist

My father on top of Camel's Hump
when he was 86 years old
*Photo by Deborah Moran, October 5, 2006*

I recently read *The Green Mountain Audubon Society and the Greening of Vermont* by Frederic O. Sargent. I was astounded to find that my father had been one of the leading environmental activists in Vermont in the 1960s and 70s. At the time, I'd thought everyone's fathers went to meetings every night. Suddenly I understood what the nonstop stream of people who paraded through our living room and down into my father's den had been doing there.

They usually arrived as we were finishing dinner. They would say hi, and my father would introduce me if I hadn't met them. Then he would say goodnight and disappear with them. After my mother put me to bed, she would join them. I would fall asleep to the sounds of voices and rustling papers, sometimes waking if the conversation got loud. Eventually someone would say, "Kari Jo is sleeping," and the voices would get soft again.

It was strange to read those people's names in the book. Names I hadn't thought of for years. Names of people who had been activists and naturalists and teachers and artists and writers. Names of people who had given their evenings and weekends and money to make Vermont into the state it is today. Because of them, Camel's Hump will be forever unblemished by ski trails and roads, Victory Bog is still a bog, there is an Audubon Nature Center in Huntington, and countless other places are still green.

I did not know that my father once waged an editorial war with a Vermont senator and publicly opposed the governor about saving a bog in the northeast part of the state that is so uniquely beautiful and wild it's referred to as the Northeast Kingdom. My father won.

I did know that he bought a mimeograph machine and kept it in his den, the same room where he carved his chickadees and held his activist meetings. I thought it was the coolest contraption ever, the way it took blank paper in one end and spat it out covered in words. I couldn't read those words yet, but I loved the rhymical thumping that shook the floor. I loved the sound of the drum rotating. I really loved the little lever that my father slid up and down to make the print darker or lighter. Sometimes he would let me slide it for him.

Once at school, I pointed out a mimeograph machine to my teacher and told her we had one in our den. She gently said that no, they were very expensive, and only people who needed to make many copies had them. I insisted that my father had one. She asked what he did for a living, and I proudly said he was a naturalist. She said, "Yes, dear," and patted my head a little worriedly.

I wondered why, the next day, my father handed me a stack of pamphlets to give to my teacher. "She said she would distribute them for me," he said. "They're for one of our day camps at the nature center. We had a nice chat on the phone last night."

I did my share of distributing pamphlets for my father too. He and his activist team jumped into action when the Burlington city government was deciding whether to build the Burlington Beltline, a road connecting the North End neighborhood to the rest of the city, bypassing North Avenue. I was dragged on a hike though wetlands that were about to be destroyed, as my father sought to educate voters about the not-ecologically-friendly decision they were being asked to make. One of his strategies involved leaving pamphlets at houses all up and down North Avenue and in the developments nearby.

On a warm evening, my parents and I canvassed our assigned area, talking to people out mowing their lawns, sitting on their porches, or riding their bikes. We rang doorbells. Sometimes doors were slammed in our faces. After one of those, my mother said, "I think that would have been worse if Kari Jo weren't here."

That gave my father an idea. The next house looked a little like the last one. It had dog poop on the lawn, which wasn't mowed, and the swing on the porch was broken. "Let's let Kari Jo ring the doorbell," my father said. "We'll just wait on the steps."

My mother protested, but my father won, and I got sent across the porch to ring the doorbell alone. When a gruff-looking man in a dirty shirt opened the door, I smiled, held out my pamphlet, and said the important bits of what I'd been hearing my father say. "Save the ducks, please. Don't build the road."

The guy looked down at me like he didn't know what to do. Then he took the pamphlet and said, "Okay, kid. Thanks." And went back inside.

After that, I got sent to a lot of houses alone.

In the end, the Beltline was built, as was the Northern Connecter a few years later, and after that the Circumferential Highway—part of it, anyway. Williston never got its Pyramid Mall, but Walmart and its box-store friends grew up there later. No, my father and the other activists didn't save everything they tried to save. But they sure were a voice in the politics of progress that threatened the greenness of our state.

Being armed with a six-year-old activist toting pamphlets sure gave them a big advantage, of course.

—*Chip Notes*, Spring 2018

# 15

# My Father and the Sea

Assateague Island beach
*Photo by Kari Jo Spear, mid 1970s*

My father was definitely a man of mountains and woods, but the sea had a piece of his heart too. I think it stemmed from the fact that his grandmother lived in Kittery, on the Maine coast. He used to visit her when he was a child, digging clams and exploring old forts. Though I rarely saw him put so much as a toe in the water, he liked to walk on the beach, and so when I would say, "How about a trip to the sea?" he'd be quick to start packing.

One year during my spring vacation from school, we headed for the island of Chincoteague, Virginia. Nearby Assateague Island has a national seashore, and that meant birds galore. Assateague also had a big draw for me—wild ponies. I loved horses of all kinds, and the thought of seeing wild ones was thrilling.

"You can see them anywhere on the island," my father said on the first morning after we got there. I kept my eyes glued to the window as we drove across the bridge from Chincoteague to Assateague. "Let's check out the auto loop."

I was all about seeing ponies without having to hike, so I eagerly scanned under the trees and along the fields as we turned onto the one-way paved road. Pretty soon we came to a marshy area, and my father pulled over. "Might be ducks," he said, a little apologetically. In a moment he was out of the car and setting up his old green spotting scope. I settled in the sun and searched the tree line with my binoculars. No ponies.

An hour later, my father got back behind the wheel, saying something about teal and a gadwall. We drove around a bend slowly. The land on both sides of the road got wetter the farther we went. Finally, at the edge of a pond, I cleared my throat and said, "Um, I thought ponies liked grass, not cattails."

My father slammed on the brakes, said "Egrets!" and was out of the car with his scope in an instant. They were pretty, I had to admit, all white and lacy feathers. While my father looked, I got a lesson through the open window about how herons had light-colored legs and egrets had dark-colored legs and look at that snowy egret! It had bright yellow feet that were kinda cool.

An hour later, we drove on. "I read that the ponies survived the shipwreck of a Spanish galleon and swam to shore and have been free ever since," I said.

My father nodded, then shrugged. "Most people think they were set free to graze on the island so people could avoid paying livestock taxes in the late seventeenth century."

"That's not very romantic," I said.

"Well, everyone agrees they've been here a long time." My father swung onto the shoulder near a large stand of phragmites. "Let's just check for rails."

I sighed.

An hour later, we were almost back to the main road. I sat up straighter and studied the higher ground. Just one last marshy area to get through. I held my breath … no.

"I hear marsh wrens!"

After another hour watching little wrens zipping through cattails and making their loud, chattering calls, we finally headed for dry land—which was where I'd be if I were a pony.

"Look at that!" My father pointed to the edge of the road.

Yes! A real, live pile of pony poop! And it smelled fresh. I hung out the window, my heart thudding.

"I bet we might see ponies on that trail," my father said, pointing to a sign that advertised a wooded walk. We pulled into a parking lot and I beat him out of the car.

Several hours later, we'd seen cardinals, woodpeckers, tufted titmice, and an unidentified hawk in the distance that disappeared before my father could get his binoculars on it. And one more pile of pony poop, not so fresh.

"Well, let's try the beach," my father said.

I had a feeling the ponies wouldn't find much to graze on where it was all sand. But the air was getting hot, and wading would feel good.

On the way, we had to drive past a salt marsh. With mudflats, since it was low tide. And that meant … "Sandpipers!"

Another hour later, I had the difference between semipalmated sandpipers and semipalmated plovers all cleared up (grayish compared to brownish), and we had agreed that peeps could be confusing.

We headed for the beach at last. I was glad to leave my shoes and socks behind. I prepared to launch into one of those wild runs across the shifting sand the way heroines in romantic movies did, after which they stood at the edge of the sea and had deep thoughts that changed the course of their lives, while the wind blew their hair.

But no. My father grabbed my arm. "Sanderlings! Don't scare them!"

So we watched crisp white birds with dark markings dash after waves, probing the wet sand with their bills until the next wave rushed in. Then they scampered back to dry sand, only to race out again as the wave fell back. After the flock had moved on, I was permitted to stand in the water. My father got the scope on a red-throated loon far out to sea.

An hour later, we walked down the shore, spotting terns, laughing gulls, and geese ("Might be brant mixed in with them!"). Finally, as the sun was setting across the dunes behind us, we headed back to the car. *Two piles of pony poop*, I thought. *Out of the whole day.*

"Well," my father said, hearing my sigh. "How about crab cakes, steamers, and birch beer for dinner?"

I was okay with crab cakes, and birch beer sounded interesting, but no way was I eating something mostly raw and slimy that was still in its shell. My father was passionate about steamers from his childhood summers in Kittery. "Fine," I said. "As long as we get ice cream on the way back to the motel."

And then we both froze at the same time. Just under the sound of the waves came a distant, rhythmic thudding from the dunes. Coming closer. We whirled, and there they were. Eight wild ponies crested a dune right behind us and galloped for the sea, chestnut and bay and black and piebald, manes and tails flying, hooves scattering the sand. They raced to the firmer footing at the edge of the waves and picked up speed, running through the water for the joy of it, sending it spraying. They played with the waves, bucking and tossing their heads, rearing and lunging in the wind. In unspoken unison, they turned and flew back up into the dunes, where they vanished into the sunset and were gone, their ghostly hoofbeats fading into the sound of the surf again.

My father and I turned to each other. Even he looked a little awestruck.

"Well," he said after a while. "I guess they are wild after all."

"Shipwreck," I said, nodding.

"Hmm." Then he nodded too. "Probably."

We started back to the car again. "Crab cakes?" I asked.

He shook his head and grinned. "Ice cream. Then crab cakes."

We both laughed. *Yeah*, I thought, *visiting the sea is pretty cool.*

—*Chip Notes*, Fall 2018

# 16
# Volcanic Mud

Vermont Mud
*Photo by Kari Jo Spear, 2019*

My father always had a calm, quiet, dignified air about him. Except, of course, when he didn't.

One late February, as we drove up Sherman Hollow Road to spend Saturday together, we noticed the road was getting muddy. Well, I noticed the car starting to sink; my father was scanning the treetops for an early robin. We made it through the soft spot all right, and I didn't think any more about it.

The day kept getting warmer, and I was happy to find a spot in the sun on Gale's old stone wall. I relaxed while my father kept an eye out for returning bluebirds and Gale puttered in her garden. (I can't be trusted not to pull up an early perennial. Birds I have a grasp of. Plants? Forget it.)

Suddenly my father lowered his binoculars. "Someone's stuck," he said. There was a strange quality to his voice I'd never heard before. It sounded almost like eagerness.

I couldn't hear a thing, but my father was so in tune with the resonance of the dirt road that he could sense a vehicle in distress long before the sound of spinning tires became audible to the rest of us. We went inside to look up the numbers of a tow truck company and the town office to report the trouble. Then I realized my father hadn't followed Gale and me in. I looked out the window to see him going down the road on his tractor.

"Going" might be the wrong word. "Galloping" was closer. I had no idea that old tractor could go so fast. And my father—well, if he'd been wearing a cowboy hat, he'd have been waving it over his head. As it was, I thought I heard him shout, "Yippee!" over the engine. He was out of sight before I could tell for sure.

Mystified, I followed in his wake. He let me catch up and hop on the back of the tractor; then we were off at full steam to the soft spot in the road.

It had turned into a full-fledged mud wallow. Not a mud bog, the kind that people play in with their four-wheel drives. This was mud at its natural muddiest. Deep, viscous tire tracks were filled with chocolate water. Fresh mud boiled up like lava from the depths of the earth. This was mud that could suck you down one limb at a time, never to be seen again.

In the middle of the thickest part was a red sports car that looked well on its way to becoming part of Sherman Hollow forever. It wasn't stuck up to its axles. Oh, no. It was mired to its *side mirrors*. The driver, a young man, stuck his head out the window and shouted, "I'm being swallowed alive!"

"You'd better get off here," my father said over his shoulder to me. "Stay clear."

Like I had any desire to get closer to a hell pit that made quicksand look like a playground accessory.

I dismounted and found a safe perch on a boulder near the tree line. My father turned the tractor around and got a chain out of his toolbox. I thought he planned to throw a line to the hapless driver and pull him out through the window before the car was fully submerged. I was wrong. My father backed the tractor right into the mud!

I leaped to my feet in horror. My father got down off the seat. I thought I'd never see him again. How was I ever going to tell Gale that he was probably in China now?

Granted, he'd certainly pick up some birds for his life list, but still! Through the earth's core was not the way to get there.

He waded in, treading from one rut's crest to the next. When he reached the car, he reached into the goop and hooked his chain to something, then strode back to the tractor and swung up into the saddle. The expression on his face as he gunned the engine was absolutely gleeful.

The engine roared deep in its throat. One big back tire spun, and mud shot up in an arc, plastering the windshield of the sports car. The tractor's front tires picked up off the ground. I screamed.

Then the tractor found its grip and strove forward, the car fishtailing behind like a kite in the wind. My father crouched, both hands on the wheel, head turned over his shoulder, riding the tractor like a bronco and shouting directions to the young man.

The mud fought valiantly to hold its prey. Long tentacles of slime burst into the air like the thrashing of a malevolent octopus. But no matter how many found their target, my father and the tractor were invincible. It was as though they were rewriting gravity itself, putting Newton to shame. Even Einstein would need to rethink his theory of relativity.

Finally, with a last, sucking shudder, the mud admitted defeat. Tractor and car burst free. The mud shrank into an evil pool, pulling a cloak of deceptive innocence over its surface to await its next victim.

My father stopped the tractor and got down. The young man got out of his now-black sports car and shook my father's hand, clearly grateful for his life. I would have been a quivering, shaking mess, but the young man was actually laughing. He looked with great respect at the old tractor as my father coiled up the chain. Together, they turned to survey the mud. I heard them replaying the scene, complete with broad gestures and lots of nods. The spatters on their clothing were like badges of bravery.

I stayed on my rock until they were done and my father looked around for me. Clearly, he'd forgotten I was even there. He motioned for me to get back on the tractor. It was completely coated with slime that looked carcinogenic. I shook my head and set out on foot for the house, keeping to the edge of the nice, safe woods. The sports car continued up the road, dripping clods of muck behind it for half a mile.

I returned to my spot in the sun and settled down with a book. My father parked the tractor not far away and got out the hose. But before he could wash down his valiant beast, his ears pricked up and he turned toward the road. Without a word, he and the tractor went galloping back to the malignant pool.

He didn't come back for the rest of the afternoon. I knew he was all right because every fifteen minutes or so, a car dripping mud came up the road. The drivers waved at me, and once someone rolled down her window and called, "Your father wants to know if you want to come and watch?"

I made the face I would have made if someone had given me boiled spinach when I asked for ice cream.

"That's what he said you'd do!" the woman called back. "But I've never seen him so happy! What is it about boys and mud?"

"I have utterly no idea," I said.

At last the sound of a truck dumping gravel into the hole to Hades reached my perch. Soon after, my father and his faithful tractor made their way up the road. I was honestly surprised he hadn't waited to make sure the town truck didn't need a pull. But when he finally reached the house, mostly mud himself, he looked a little crestfallen.

"What's wrong?" I asked. "I thought you were having a wonderful day."

"Oh, I was," he said quickly. "It's just, well—it's all filled in now. I was kinda hoping to see what my car would do with it when it was time to take you home. It's all about where you put your tires, you know? I think we could have made it."

He laughed at my expression, and I realized he'd gotten me—again.

—*Chip Notes*, Summer 2019

# 17

# My Father and the Camp

Camp at twilight.
Lake Champlain, Colchester, Vermont
*Photo by Kari Jo Spear, 2016*

The Adirondack Mountains from camp
*Photo by Kari Jo Spear, 2019*

One of the best things my family ever did, they did before I was born. And it's had a lasting influence on me.

Back in the late 1950s, everyone then in the family— my parents, my mother's parents, two of my mother's aunts, and my mother's brother and his wife—chipped in and bought a piece of property on the eastern side of Lake Champlain. For several years, they had rented a camp on the lake for a week or so during the summer, and they'd enjoyed it so much that they thought it would great to have their own place.

At the same time, Interstate 89 punched through the family farm, thanks to eminent domain, and they lost a lot of land. However, they gained a lot of lumber from the red pines that had to be cut. I can imagine the glint in my father's eye as he thought about what he could do with all that wood. (Besides carve it, of course.)

So the way I heard it, my parents spent a lot of time exploring the lakeshore by canoe, looking for the perfect spot for their camp. They found it one day by landing on a rock and scrambling up a narrow cleft in a thirty-foot dolomite cliff. At the top, they found a lovely spot with lots of ledges and moss and hardy cedar trees. It faced an absolutely spectacular view of six miles of open water, beyond which lay South Hero. The Adirondack Mountains rose in the background like distant purple sentinels. The sun set while they were there, and the breathtaking beauty of it told them they'd found the spot they were looking for.

Their luck held when they located the owner of the land. He was completely amenable to them carving out the chunk they wanted. Not only that, but when two sets of family friends saw the property, they instantly bought land on either side. Over the course of the next few summers, the three families all pitched in and helped build each other's camps.

My father designed our camp to take advantage of the contours of the land, building into the side of a ledge rather than disturbing the natural setting. The downstairs is one large room with lofty, open-rafter ceilings. The entire front is windows that take in the view, and there is a screened-in porch at the far end. Two stairways lead to four bedrooms, with windows carefully placed for cross-ventilation.

My favorite part of the building is the fingerprints left unintentionally on the underside of the roof boards, by fingers stained with the brown stain they used on the outside. I love to lie in bed and look up at them, guessing at whose prints they are.

My father made a path to the rock where they first landed. There he built a wooden dock and a ladder leading down into the cool water. The dock was perfect for jumping off, especially if I got up a good head of steam and my parents weren't around to discourage me from running across the planks.

There were birds galore—great crested flycatchers with their gravelly calls, red-eyed vireos that sang all summer, scarlet tanagers looking like Christmas ornaments in the cedars, loons calling in the misty mornings, and a pair of phoebes that claimed the camp as theirs the very first summer. They built a nest under an overhang near the door.

My father created a beautiful fireplace with rocks taken from the space he blasted for the dock. It's mostly made of dolomite, which is a lovely pinkish color and has lots of red veins forming fascinating shapes within each piece. Unfortunately, the fireplace never worked well—it smokes when the wind is from the north, which is when one would usually want a fire. But it has always seemed like artwork to me, and I can't imagine camp without its solid presence in the center. It's the heart of camp.

Like the fireplace, something else about camp never quite worked out—my parents' marriage. My father moved out the summer I was ten. The reasons why were between my parents, not me. But my world became hollow and empty while we struggled to rearrange things we'd thought were permanent.

There were other changes. My grandmother and one of my great-aunts passed away. My uncle and his wife moved to California. My grandfather was always busy on his farm, and my remaining great-aunt spent most of her time in her apartment in Montpelier. So camp became my mother's—and mine.

At first, it seemed very lonely. It was hard walking the dirt road without my father there to point out birds. I even missed him telling me to be quiet when he was trying to spot something high in the treetops (which was most of the time). But though things were sad, there was never any doubt in my mind that both my parents loved me dearly. I think now that only seeing my father on weekends and during vacations made us cherish our time together more. It sounds cliched, but I believe it is true. The divorce also brought Gale into my life—much later, after everyone's lives had settled down into their new patterns—which was a very good thing.

Sixty years on, camp itself hasn't changed much. It now has internet, a filter system so we can drink lake water, and a washer and drier. These make life a whole lot easier. The walls still glow with the warmth of red pine, the windows still look straight to the Adirondacks, and the descendants of the phoebes still nest under the overhang near the door. The fingerprints still hold their silent mysteries on the inside of the roof.

To my excitement, a pair of peregrine falcons have recently chosen to nest on the dolomite cliff face. Though their nest site isn't visible from the camp, one of their favorite perches is in a pine partway down our path to the water. Their cries often fill the camp with the harsh but beautiful sound of the freedom of the skies. Everyone I tell about them says how wonderful it is that they are there. I agree—and I'm not surprised. My father picked out the spot for the camp. Why wouldn't peregrine falcons nest nearby?

# 18
# Remembrance: Tales of My Father

My father at the
Green Mountain Audubon Center
*Photo by Kari Jo Spear, mid 1970s*

In place of a regular Carver's Daughter installment, I want to offer a few tidbits of information about my father that most people probably don't know. Bear in mind that they are family stories and may have been embellished through the years. (But not by me, *of course!*)

Our name shouldn't be Spear. My great-grandmother, Julia Spear, eloped with a man from Canada named Ovitt, and disappeared for an entire year. One day she reappeared on her parents' doorstep with a newborn baby, simply saying that she was divorced. She took back the name Spear for herself and her baby, who was my grandfather, the first Robert N. Spear.

My father did not grow up in Vermont, though he was born here. He was raised until he was about sixteen years old in Wyben, Massachusetts. His family had moved there so that his mother could continue teaching after she got married. Vermont had a law then that only single women could teach school.

My father was kidnapped when he was a baby. One day his mother was sitting on a train platform, with my father in a basket at her feet. A woman passing by snatched him, basket and all, and raced off into the crowd. His mother tore after them, screaming. Fortunately, some people farther down the platform were able to stop the woman. She was, as they said back then, "mentally deranged," and had stolen my father because he was such a cute baby. He slept through the entire experience.

My grandmother was my father's first teacher, in a one-room schoolhouse.

After her death, my grandfather moved to Colchester with his teenage son and daughter. My father became friends with Charles Smith, and the two boys explored Lake Champlain and the surrounding woods and fields together. Their role model was Yan, the hero of Ernest Thompson Seton's *Two Little Savages*, a popular boy's book of the time. They pitched a tent midway between their houses and slept in it all summer. They were avid ice skaters in the winter and built their own iceboat—which, my father said, "went like a bat out of hell." I'm sure they had no safety equipment.

One winter, a Model T broke through the lake ice and sank near their fishing shanty. A man struggled to the surface, and the boys shoved their sled out to him. He grabbed on and they pulled him to safety—but he had a heart attack and died before they could get him into the warmth of the shanty. Decades later, my father made me promise never to ride in a car on the ice. I never will.

My father and Charles each had a daughter the same year. Helen and I were friends before we started school, and we have been friends ever since.

My father claimed to have paddled the first canoe on Malletts Bay in recent times. It was made of black canvas stretched over a wooden frame. It weighted about a thousand pounds when dry and twice that wet, and he claimed it was the best paddling canoe he ever had. Drivers on Lakeshore Drive used to stop and stare at him in his funny boat with points at both ends.

As a young man, my father frequented a roller-skating rink at Clarey's Bayside in Colchester. Years later, when Gale accepted an invitation to a roller-skating party for herself and my father, she was afraid he would be in for a miserable afternoon. But when she looked up from lacing her skates, my father was already on the floor, weaving between people as he skated backwards on one foot. He had a huge grin on his face, of course.

My father once had a horse named Ned. He also had a cat he loved dearly, so much that after it died, he vowed he would never have another pet. He never did. (Though he was known to cuddle Gale's cat Hussy quite a bit.)

As a boy, my father smoked everything he could get hold of. When cigarettes were too expensive, he smoked corn silk, which he said was all right, or rolled-up wild grapevine, which was awful. Perhaps that was what cured him of the smoking habit before he became an adult.

He built himself a darkroom, learned taxidermy and astronomy from books, made two guitars and a mandolin, played them all, and could cut down a tree with an ax, dropping it exactly where he wanted it every time.

My father was bullied in high school. He was young for his grade—small, shy, and smart—and therefore a target for tough Winooski boys. After he graduated, he vowed he would never set foot in another school as a student. He pretty much never did, aside from a few night classes in math at UVM and his training in the navy later.

He worked in a sawmill and on the Blakely Farm in Colchester, plowing and haying with a team of horses. He cut ice with a crosscut saw on the lake. He always said that he preferred the end on top of the ice, when he could get it.

During World War II, he enlisted in the navy, against his father's wishes. The result of his math tests landed him in Chicago for the duration of the war, putting his skills to use meeting the desperate need for radar development to detect German planes and U-boats. It wasn't what he'd hoped for; he wanted to follow in the footsteps of his great-grandfather and hero, Alonzo Spear, who fought in every major battle of the Civil War. But in time, he realized the importance of his work and reflected on the lives he'd helped to save. Still, I'm sure he always regretted that he hadn't had a chance to take out Hitler with a well-thrown ax.

Radar experts became critical crew members onboard ships by the end of the war. My father had just been assigned to a ship in the South Pacific when the United States dropped the atomic bombs. Once, self-righteously, I criticized our country for causing such violence. My father quietly told me that if the United States hadn't dropped the bombs, I probably would not exist. Neither would the Birds of Vermont Museum. I kept my mouth shut about that afterward.

While he was in the navy, my father was good friends with Jeffrey Hunter, who became an actor after the war and played Captain Christopher Pike in the original *Star Trek* pilot episode, among other roles.

My father used to have his own Boy Scout troop. He was also a magnet for troubled teenagers. When one parent thanked him from the bottom of her heart for turning her child's life around, he shrugged and said, "Well, I just had him help me clear a trail." Or dig a pond. Or spot a bird. Just that.

My father almost blew up a man once. When he wanted to create a way down to the lakeshore from the property where he and my mother were building our camp, he bought some dynamite. He drilled into the ledge, planted the charge, and set it off. Rock rained down into the lake.

And a man who had been quietly fishing in a rowboat shot out from behind a tiny island just offshore. My father said the guy was all right, but he was madder than a hornet.

My father was married twice before he met Gale—first to a woman named Eileen, and then to my mother, Sally Stalker Spear. I am his only child. He wanted to name me Robin, whether I was a boy or a girl. My mother wanted to name me Joelle. He thought that was too unusual, so they settled for Karen Joelle. But the first time he saw me, he said, "That's not a Karen Joelle. That's a Kari Jo." The nickname stuck. I was never quite sure what he meant.

My parents separated when I was ten and later divorced. I only saw my father on weekends or school vacations for the rest of my childhood.

My father was the founding director of the Green Mountain Audubon Nature Center.

My father hunted deer until, as he put it, he "grew out of it."

My father voted Republican until, as he put it, he "wised up."

He worked as a salesman at Sears for a short time before moving on to a career at General Electric, doing further work with radar.

He disliked coffee and alcohol, except for an occasional beer.

He could hardly swim a stroke and hated to even get his big toe wet.

He was a lousy cook. Aside from making really good cheeseburgers, all he ever fixed for himself was a can of Dinty Moore beef stew. And ice cream, of course.

He was so squeamish that he used to leave movies during gory parts. Once when I cut my finger, he had to go sit in the shade while I put on a Band-Aid.

He could mentally fight every battle of the Civil War and tell you where all the Vermont troops had stood in each one. He was also an expert on the American Revolution, which had far simpler battles.

He designed and built a house, a camp, a museum, Gale's retreat, countless bird blinds, and a bridge that withstood a flood that took out all the ground around it.

He sat through *The Nutcracker* ballet at least fifteen times, doing grandfather duty. And honestly said he liked it.

He occasionally traveled, driving across the country from one national park to the next, giving all cities a wide berth. He went to the South American tropics several times, but never farther from home than that. I did hear him say once that he'd like to go to Africa.

He had a unique sense of humor and delivered all his lines as a straight, deadpan part of his normal conversation. To a group of volunteers he was training to work in the nature center's sugar orchard, I heard him say, "Audubon only allows us to run over three kids with the tractor per year. Choose them wisely."

To a student who pointed at a fat, furry woodchuck under the birdfeeders and asked what it was, my father said, "That's a chipmunk. They lose their stripes when they get that big."

He never went anywhere without his binoculars, not even in an ambulance to the hospital. They see peregrine falcons around there, you know.

I asked, when I was a child and first grappling with the idea of death, if he would ever die. He told me yes, but not for a long, long time. He was right.

In the end, when we were told he had only months to live, he did things his own way and wrapped everything up in three days. I was with him when he passed. He did it with the least amount of fuss possible, a recording of birds' songs playing in the background.

A few days later, Gale and I scattered most of his ashes at his favorite places around the museum grounds, as he'd requested. I sprinkled the rest from his bridge over the museum's brook, knowing they would wash down through the Audubon Nature Center and eventually into the lake, where he'd once paddled his odd boat with points at both ends and raced an iceboat into the stars.

One other thing I know for certain: as a friend said, he will have already added a Labrador duck and a passenger pigeon to his life list.

—*Chip Notes*, Winter 2015

*Photo by Bob Spear, date unknown*

# Afterword

I hope you've enjoyed *The Carver's Daughter*.

In case you're wondering, I did grow up to be a writer, and I've got five novels in print at the moment (winter 2020). They've been published under a pen name to protect my privacy while I was working in a public high school. I got married and have two grown daughters, neither of whom carve but both of whom are very involved in the arts: one is a music teacher and performer, and the other is a dancer. So I can safely say that my father passed on the artistic gene, though it morphed a bit. I'm still working on my life list, still canoeing, and still taking photographs. I am on the board of directors at the museum. Life is good.

I encourage everyone to visit the Birds of Vermont Museum in Huntington, Vermont. The website is www.birdsofvt.org, where you can find more information, including driving directions. If you become a member, you'll get lots of benefits, like free admission and several installments of *Chip Notes* throughout the year. That way, you can keep up with the latest Carver's Daughter ... articles? essays? vignettes?

You can find me on the internet at: carversdaughter.blogspot.com

Thanks for reading!

CPSIA information can be obtained
at www.ICGtesting.com
Printed in the USA
BVHW061241150720
583707BV00005B/211

9 781735 079912